Beginning ROCK GUITAR FOR KIDS

A Fun, Easy Approach To Playing Today's Rock Guitar Styles!

by Jimmy Brown

ISBN 978-0-7935-2017-6

HAL•LEONARD®

Visit Hal Leonard Online at
www.halleonard.com

Contact us:
Hal Leonard
7777 West Bluemound Road
Milwaukee, WI 53213
Email: info@halleonard.com

In Europe, contact:
Hal Leonard Europe Limited
42 Wigmore Street
Marylebone, London, W1U 2RN
Email: info@halleonardeurope.com

In Australia, contact:
Hal Leonard Australia Pty. Ltd.
4 Lentara Court
Cheltenham, Victoria, 3192 Australia
Email: info@halleonard.com.au

Photography and Book Design by Melissa Brown Blaeuer
Music Typography: Darren West

Contents

About The Author

Jimmy Brown is an experienced player and teacher in the New York City area. As Music Editor for **Guitar World**, **Guitar School, Guitar Legends** and **Country Guitar** magazines, he regularly interviews the world's greatest players and explains their techniques in detail. Jimmy holds a Bachelor of Music degree and has written numerous articles, columns, and books on rock guitar styles. He continues to play live dates both professionally and for the sheer thrill of it!

To The Student

This is the book you've been looking for—a fun, easy introduction to playing the guitar that's oriented towards *today's* kid. Unlike other beginner guitar courses that show you how to play songs like "Twinkle, Twinkle, Little Star" and "This Old Man," **Beginning Rock Guitar For Kids** features cool **riffs** and **licks** that sound like *Metallica, Guns N' Roses* and *Nirvana.*

This book covers the fundamentals you need to know to get started, such as how to hold the guitar, basic left- and right-hand technique, tuning your guitar and music notation, and gets you jamming on some simple, but cool, rhythm and lead patterns. To make sure you're playing everything properly, I recommend that you use this book with a guitar teacher.

Practicing

Playing the guitar should be fun. It shouldn't be like school. To become a good guitarist, however, you have to practice regularly. It's better to practice for just a few minutes a day than to cram all your practicing into one long session once or twice a week. Try to stick to a regular practice schedule, but don't feel bad if you miss a day every now and then. Go at your own pace and have fun!

The Basics

The Electric Guitar

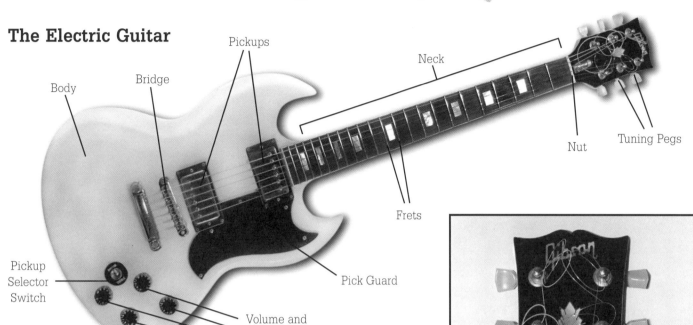

Pickups

Bridge

Body

Neck

Nut

Tuning Pegs

Frets

Pickup Selector Switch

Pick Guard

Volume and Tone Controls for Each Pickup

Amplifier

Speaker

Mono Guitar Cable With 1/4" Plugs

The Guitar Has Six Strings

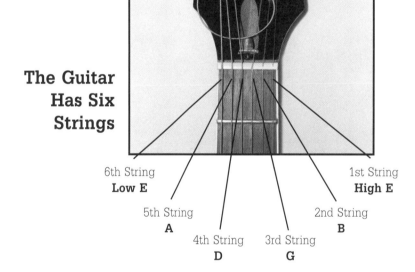

6th String
Low E

5th String
A

4th String
D

3rd String
G

2nd String
B

1st String
High E

Amplifier Control Knobs

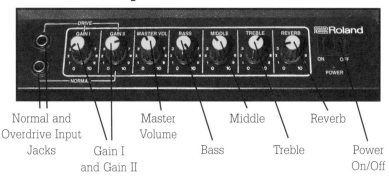

Normal and Overdrive Input Jacks

Gain I and Gain II

Master Volume

Bass

Middle

Treble

Reverb

Power On/Off

How To Hold The Guitar

Sitting...

...and Standing

Holding A Pick

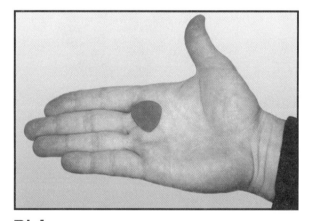

Pick

The correct way to hold a pick (pointed tip facing strings).

The Downstroke

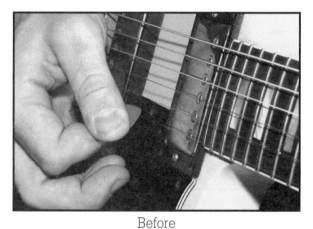

Before

After

Drag the pick downward across the string.

Tuning Your Guitar

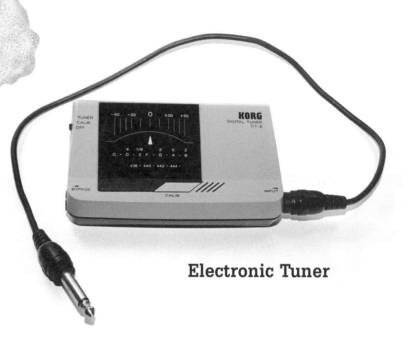

ALWAYS TUNE YOUR GUITAR BEFORE YOU PLAY! The easiest way to do this is with an electronic tuner.

Electronic Tuner

Tuning The Strings To A Keyboard

The arrows point to the white piano keys that correspond to the guitar's six open strings.

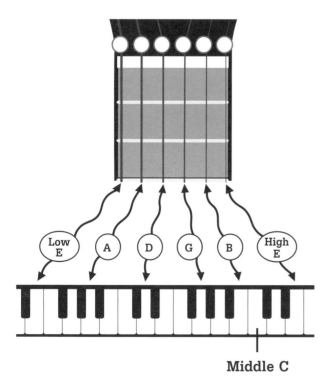

Low E   A   D   G   B   High E

Middle C

Tuning The Strings To Each Other

The black circles show where to press down with a finger and the white circles show the string to play "open" (unpressed) while turning the tuning peg to get the same note. Begin by tuning the 5th string to the 6th string, then tune the 4th string to the 5th string, the 3rd string to the 4th, and so on.

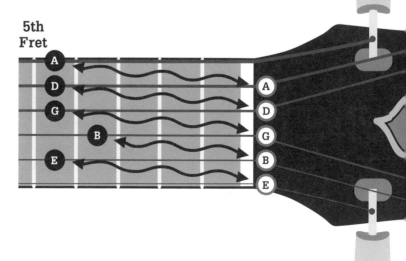

5th Fret

A
D
G
B
E

A
D
G
B
E

Music Notation

Figure 1 The musical staff.

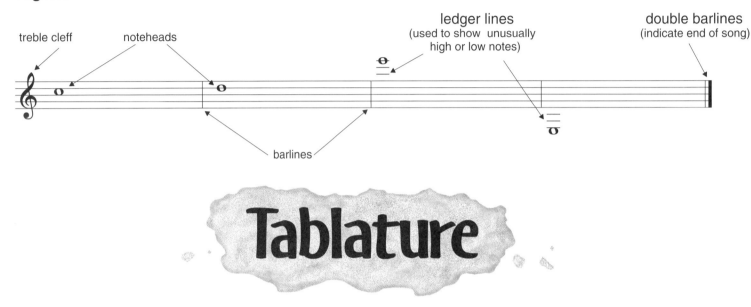

treble cleff
noteheads
ledger lines
(used to show unusually high or low notes)
double barlines
(indicate end of song)
barlines

Tablature

Figure 2 Tablature illustrates the guitar's six strings.

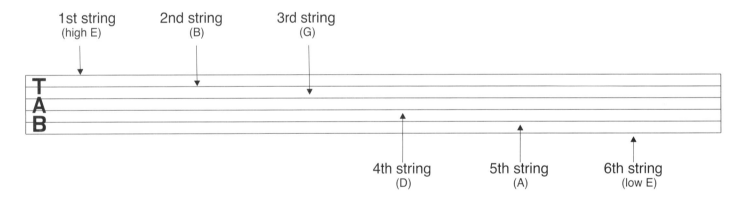

1st string
(high E)
2nd string
(B)
3rd string
(G)
4th string
(D)
5th string
(A)
6th string
(low E)

Numbers represent frets.

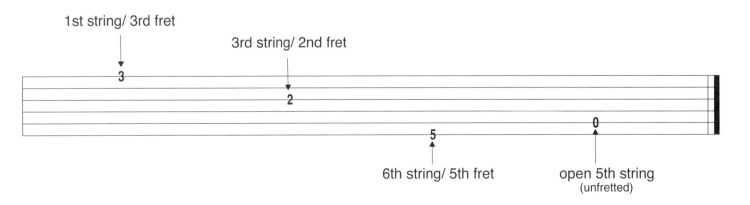

1st string/ 3rd fret
3rd string/ 2nd fret
6th string/ 5th fret
open 5th string
(unfretted)

Basic Rhythms

Figure 3 The musical staff with tablature.

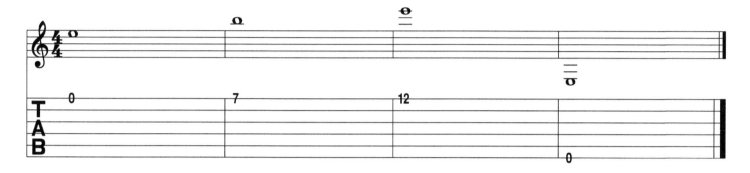

Figure 4 $\frac{4}{4}$ **time signature** tells you there are four beats in each measure.

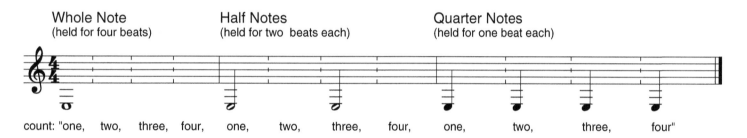

Whole Note
(held for four beats)

Half Notes
(held for two beats each)

Quarter Notes
(held for one beat each)

count: "one,   two,   three,   four,   one,   two,   three,   four,   one,   two,   three,   four"

Notes On The Low E String

Figure 5 Each note is pictured, with its notation and tablature below. Be sure to place your finger *behind the fret*.

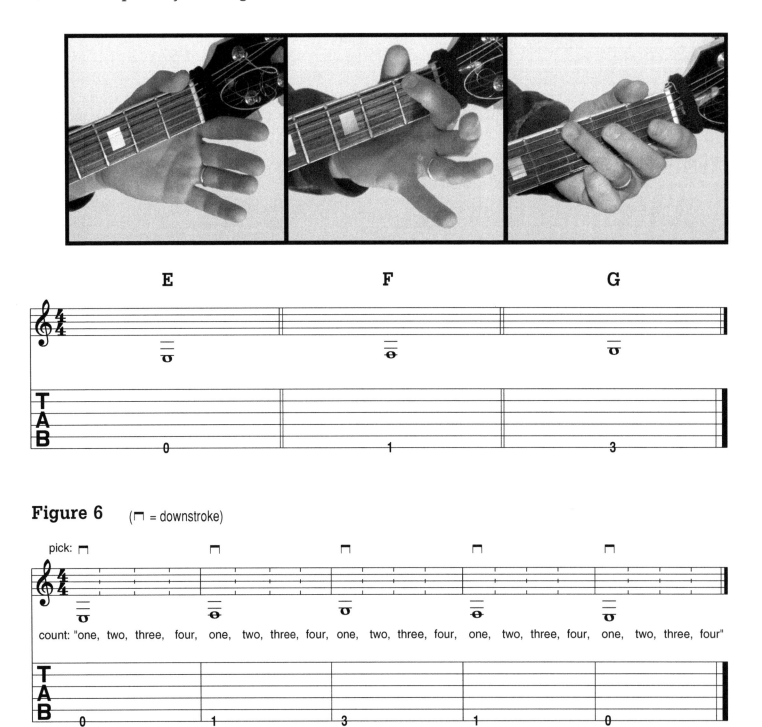

Figure 6 (⊓ = downstroke)

Figure 7

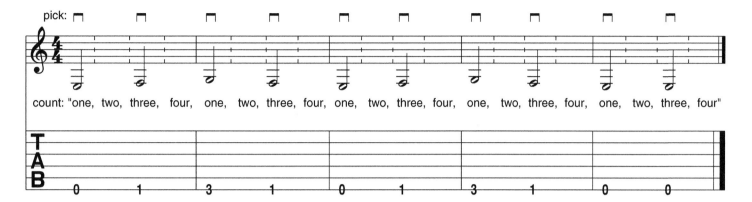

Figure 8

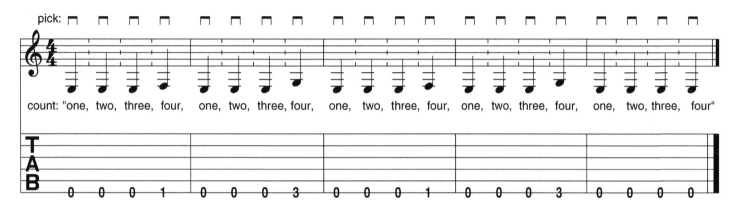

Figure 9

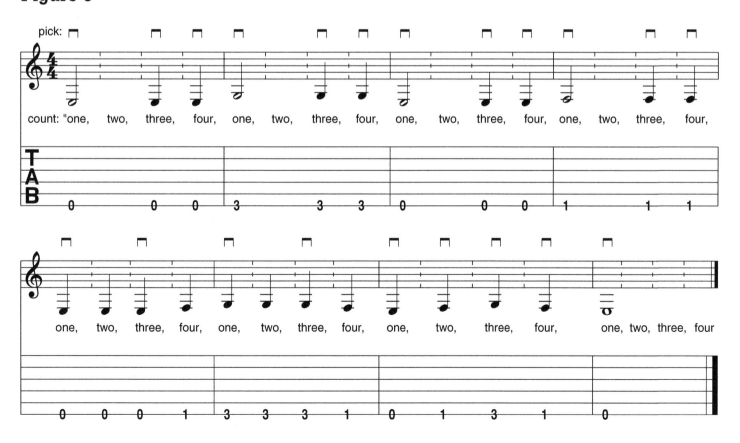

Notes On The A String

Figure 10 Each note is pictured, with its notation and tablature below.

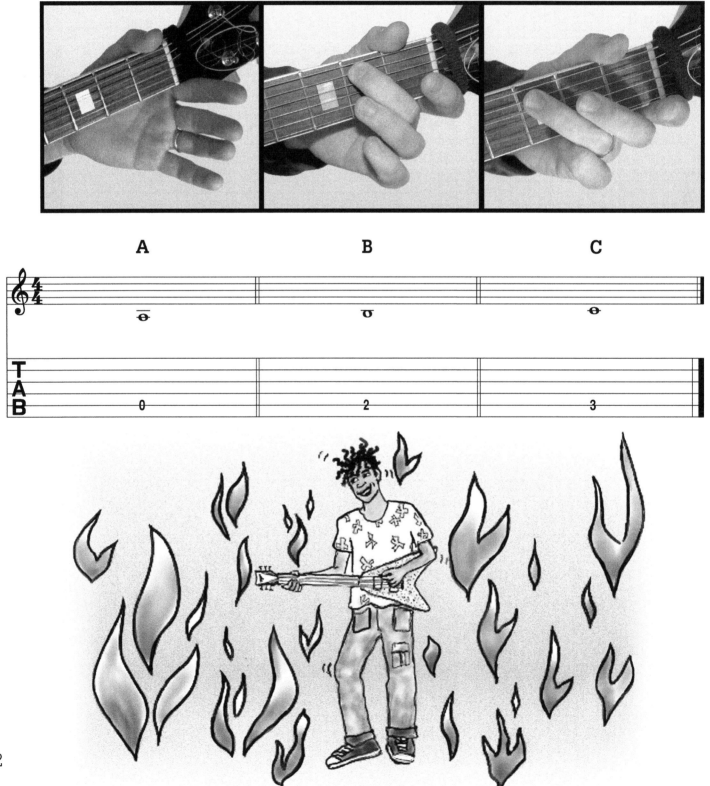

Figure 11

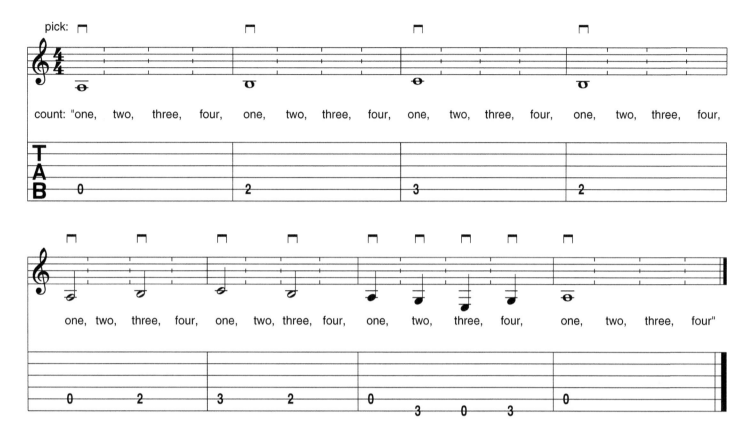

Figure 12

Figure 13

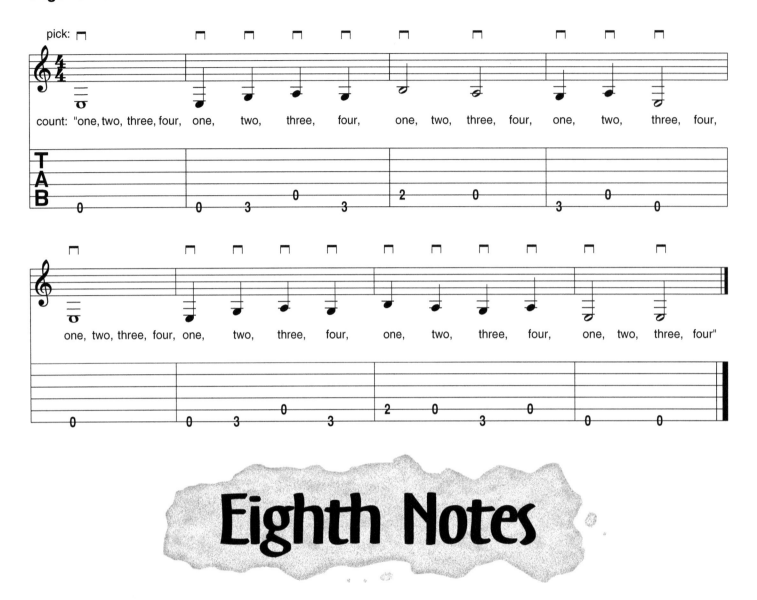

Eighth Notes

A measure of 4/4 can also be divided into eight **eighth notes**. Each eighth note is held for half a beat.

Figure 14

count: "one - and, two - and, three - and, four - and, one - and, two - and, three - and, four - and"

Eighth notes are used by every rock band from *Stone Temple Pilots* to *Megadeth* to *Pearl Jam*. Let's play some eighth notes now.

Figure 15

Figure 16

Figure 17

Figure 18

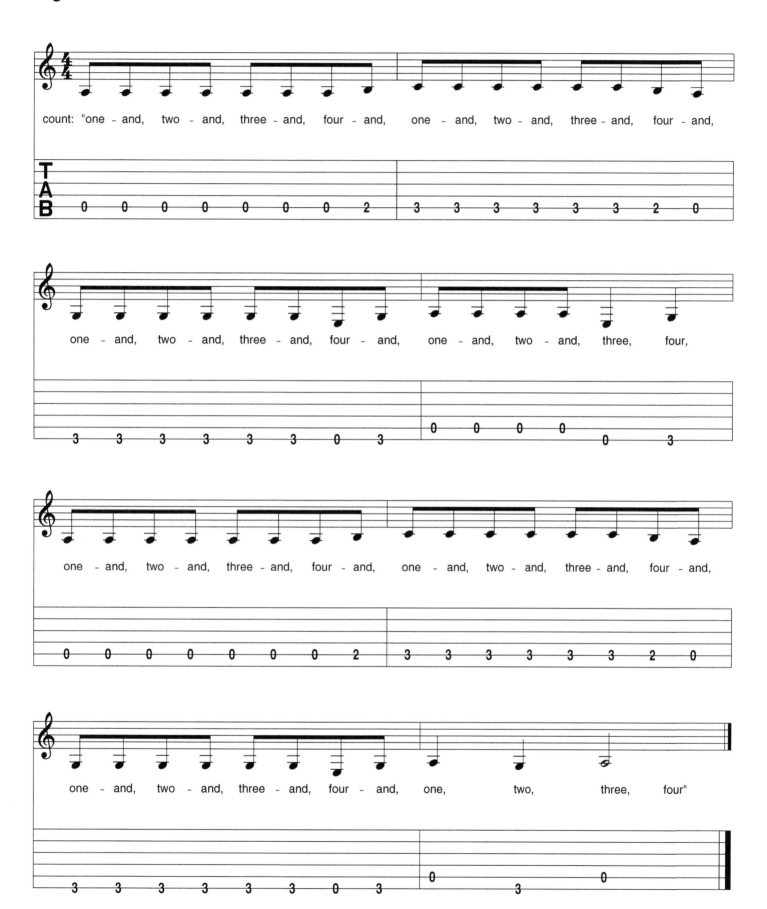

Notes On The D and G Strings

Figure 19   Each note is pictured, with its notation and tablature below.

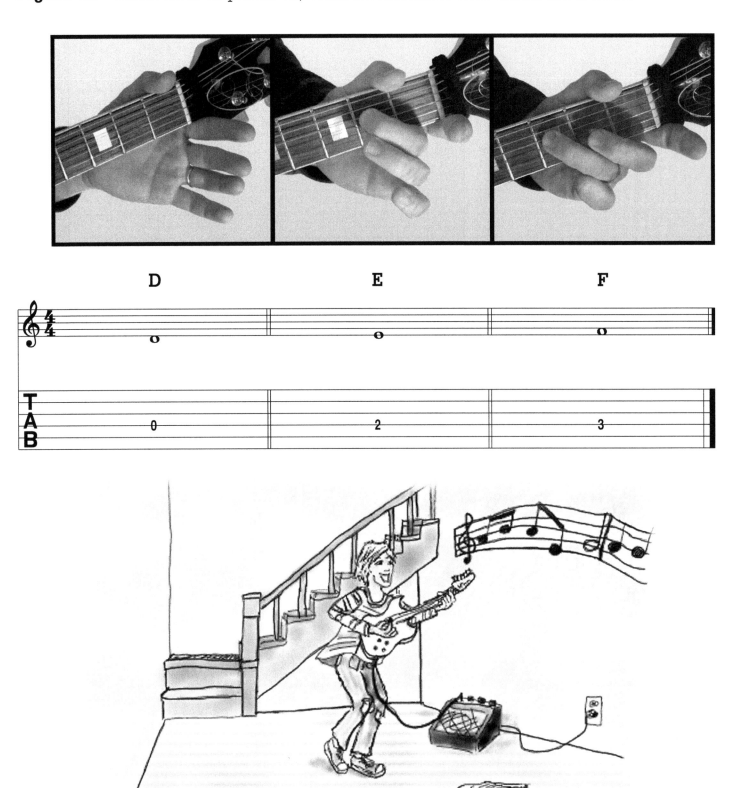

Figure 20 Each note is pictured, with its notation and tablature below.

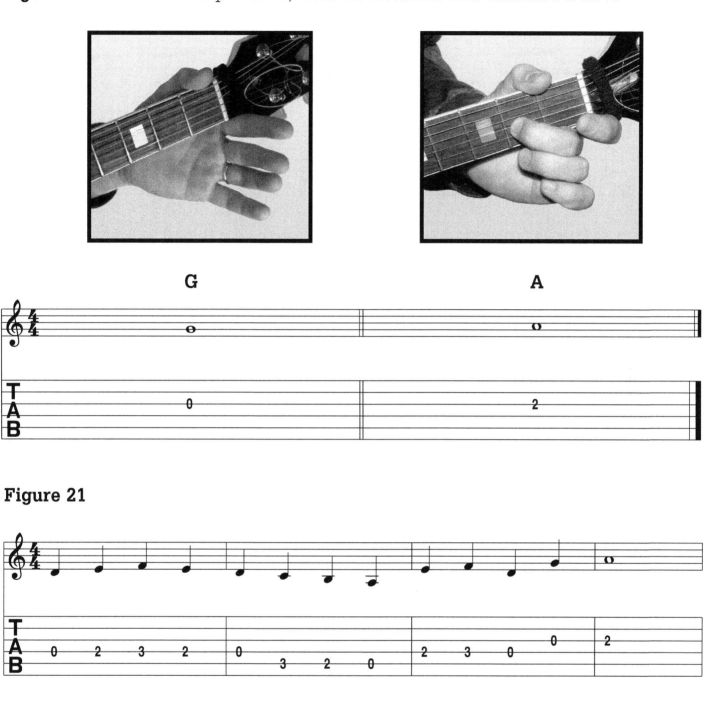

Figure 22

Power Chords

Figure 23 Here are three **power chords**. They're called power chords because they sound very powerful, like a motorcycle engine. To play each power chord, **strum** both strings using a single downstroke.

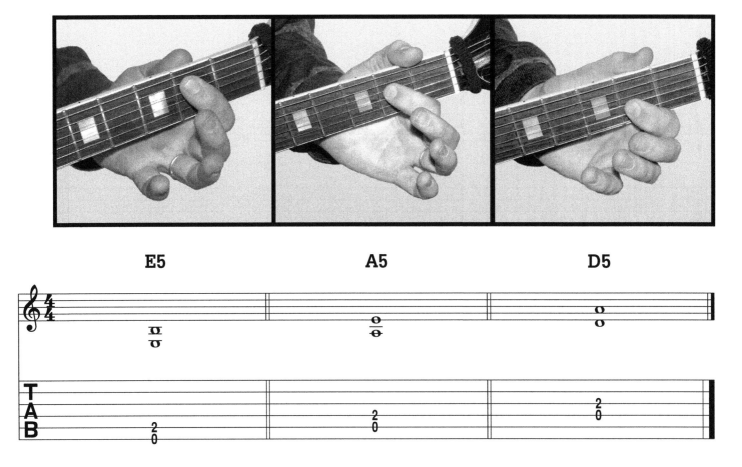

E5   A5   D5

Let's practice switching power chords now.

Figure 24

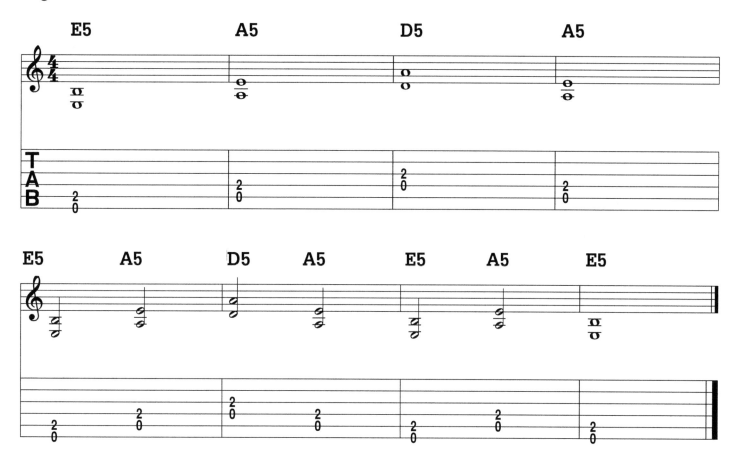

Figure 25

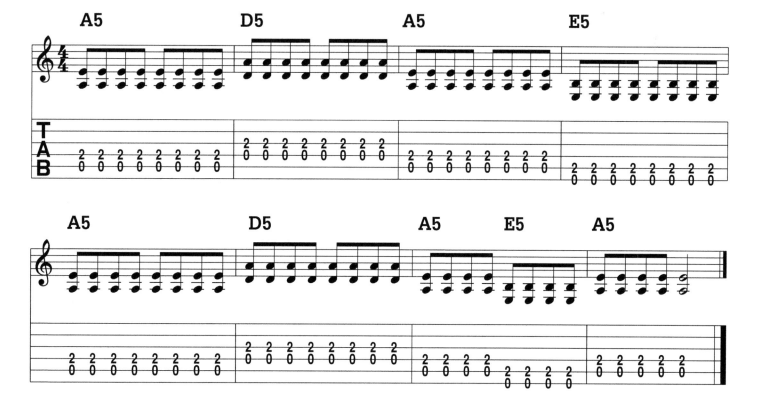

Here are some cool **riffs** that use power chords and single notes.

Figure 26

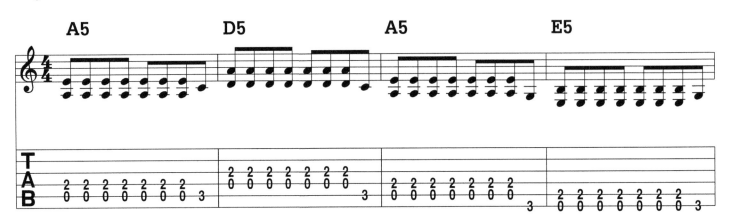

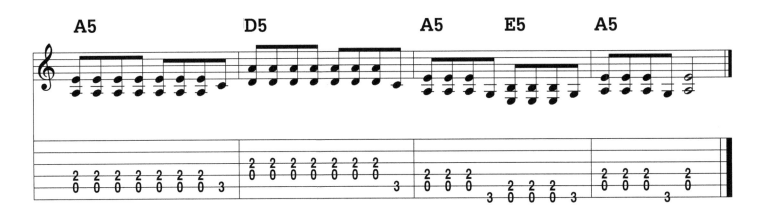

Figure 27

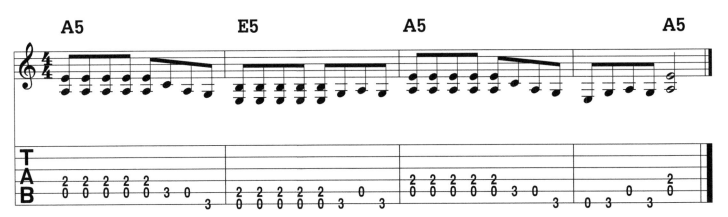

Figure 28

Palm Muting

Palm muting ("P.M.") is a technique where you lightly rest your right palm on the strings as you pick.

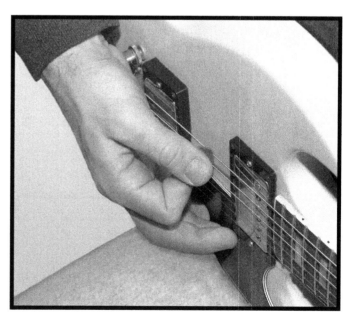

Palm muting helps make your playing sound cleaner and "tighter" and gives your picking a "chunky," pumping quality that's great for rock. Let's try strumming some power chords now using palm muting.

Figure 29

Here's a riff that uses palm muting.

Figure 30

Accents

An **accent** (>) placed under or over a note tells you to emphasize that note by picking it harder than normal. The following riff combines palm muting with accents.

Figure 31

Figure 32

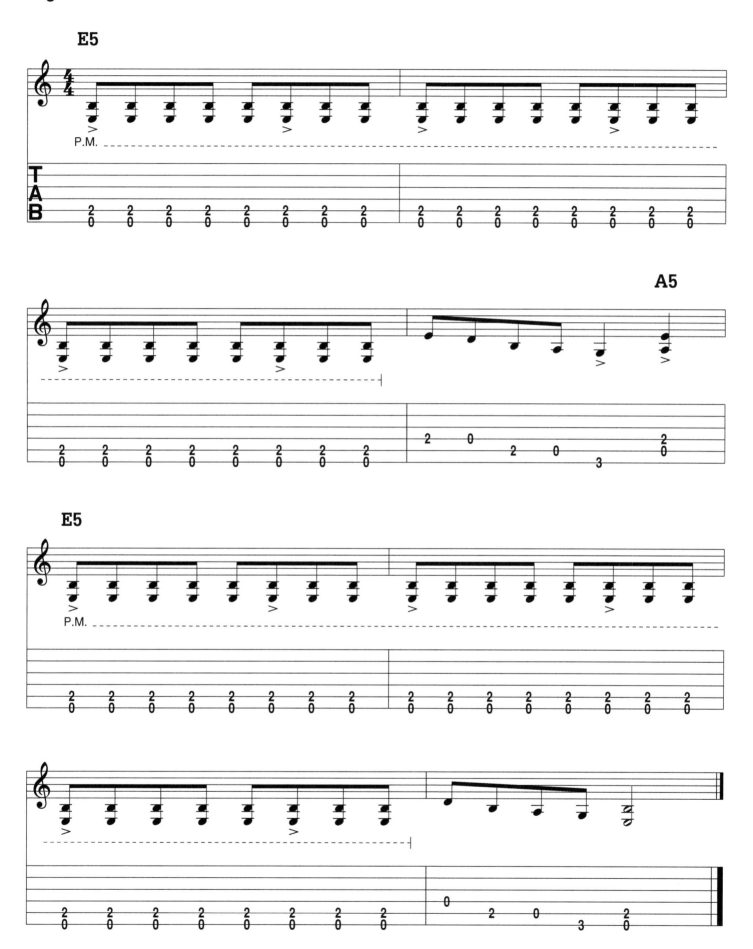

Accidentals

Accidentals are musical symbols that tell you to raise or lower a note. An accidental remains in effect until the end of a measure.

♯ = **sharp** tells you to *raise* a note one fret   ♭ = **flat** tells you to *lower* a note one fret   ♮ = **natural** cancels a sharp or flat

Figure 33   Playing Up and Down One String

Figure 34

Power Chord Extensions

These **power chord extensions** are used by many rock bands like the *Black Crowes*, the *Spin Doctors* and *Van Halen*.

Figure 35

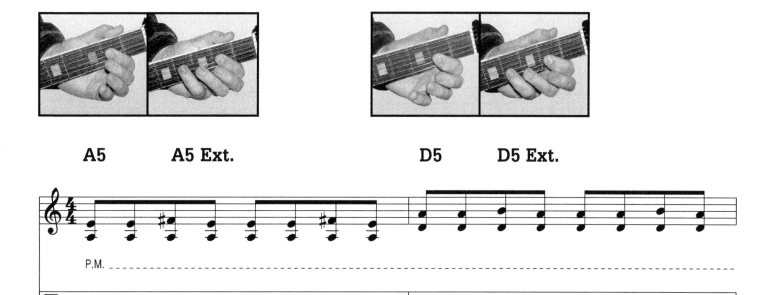

A5   A5 Ext.   D5   D5 Ext.

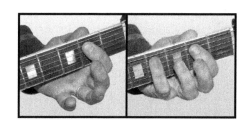

A5   A5 Ext.   E5   E5 Ext.

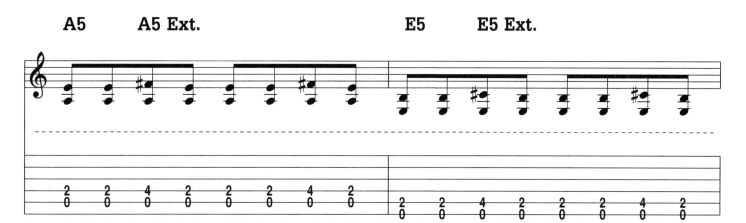

Figure 35 (continued)

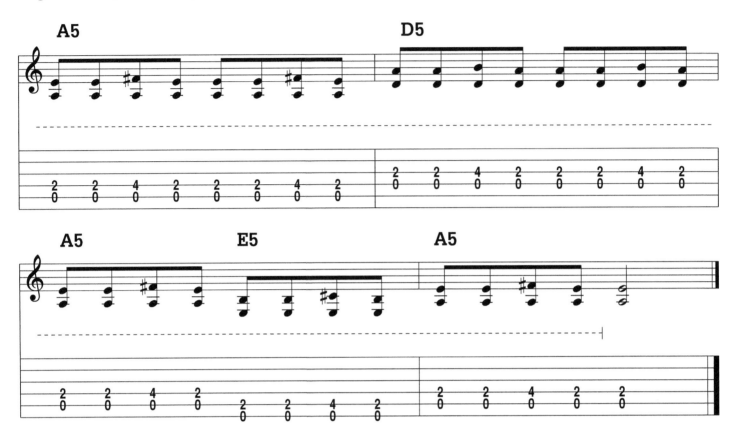

Here's a riff that uses these power chord extensions.

Figure 36

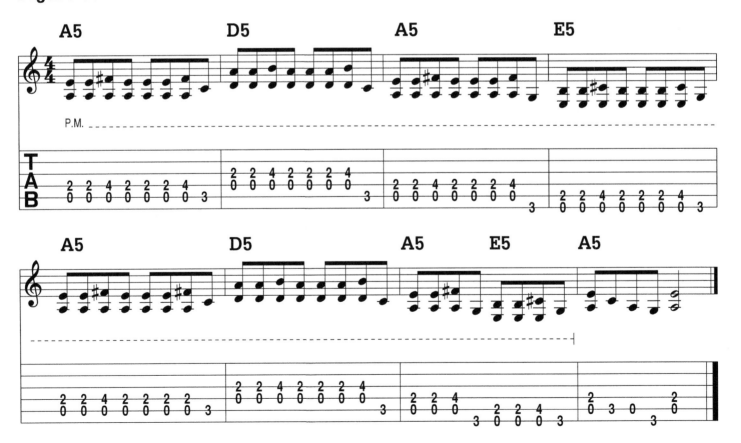

The 12-Bar Blues Progression

The 12-bar blues progression is used in countless rock songs such as *Led Zeppelin's* "Rock And Roll," *Van Halen's* "Ice Cream Man" and *Stevie Ray Vaughan's* "Love Struck Baby."

Figure 37   12-Bar Blues Progression in A

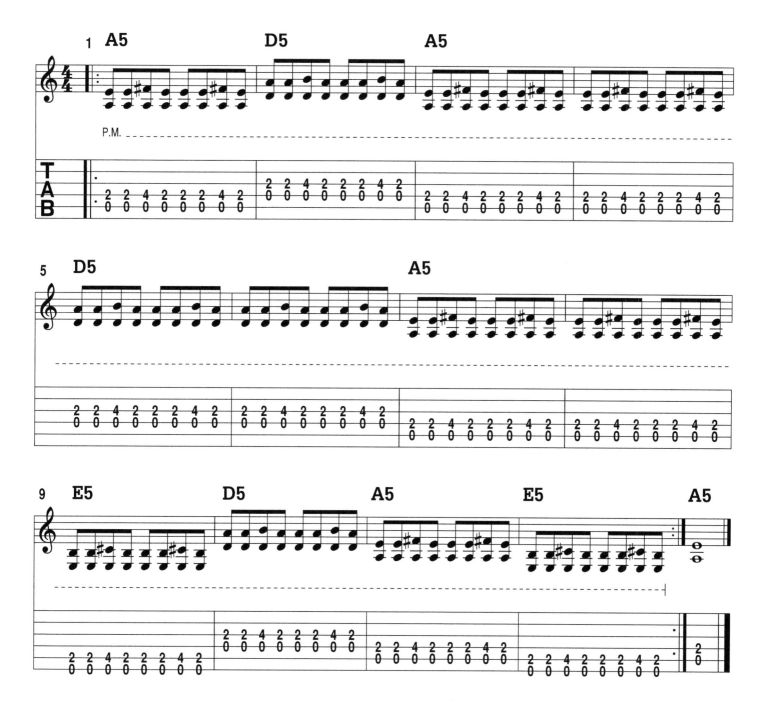

Playing Lead Guitar

So far we've covered the basics of **rhythm guitar**, which involves playing riffs. Now we're going to explore the exciting world of **lead guitar**, which involves playing solos.

Becoming a great rock lead guitarist requires lots of practicing, listening, and experience playing with other musicians. The first step, however, is to learn the **A minor-pentatonic scale** shown below.

Figure 38   Notice that each A note is circled. A is considered the **root note** of the scale.

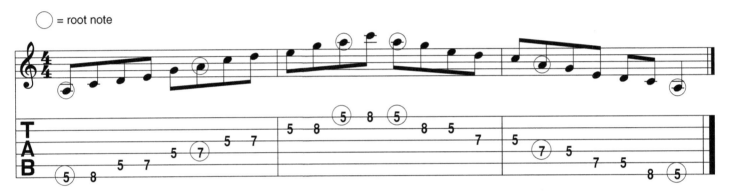

Figure 39   Play the A5 power chord and the A minor-pentatonic scale shown below. Listen to the way they "fit" together.

The A minor-pentatonic scale can be used to play cool **licks** like these.

Figure 40

Figure 41

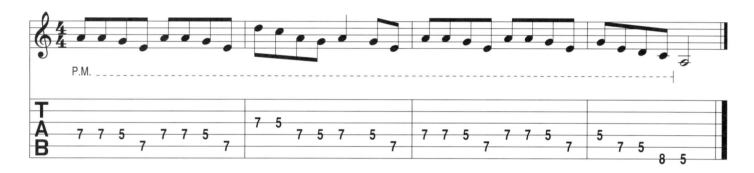

Figure 42

Jamming

The best way to learn how to solo is to **jam** with other musicians. Jamming means playing whatever comes into your head while someone else plays a repeated riff. Jamming teaches you how to **play by ear** and enables you to work on *applying* everything you've learned in a real musical situation. Try to jam as often as possible. You'll be amazed at how quickly your playing will improve!

To get started, have a friend play any of the riffs shown in *Figures 11, 12, 15, 18, 25, 26, 27, 28, 30, 31, 35, 36* or *37* while you improvise a solo using the A minor-pentatonic scale shown in *Figure 38*. If no one else is available to accompany you, record yourself playing the riffs, then solo along with the recording.

Here's a sample guitar solo played over a 12-bar blues progression in A. Have a friend play the rhythm part (Gtr. 2) while you play the lead part (Gtr. 1), then switch roles.

Figure 43   12-Bar Blues Jam

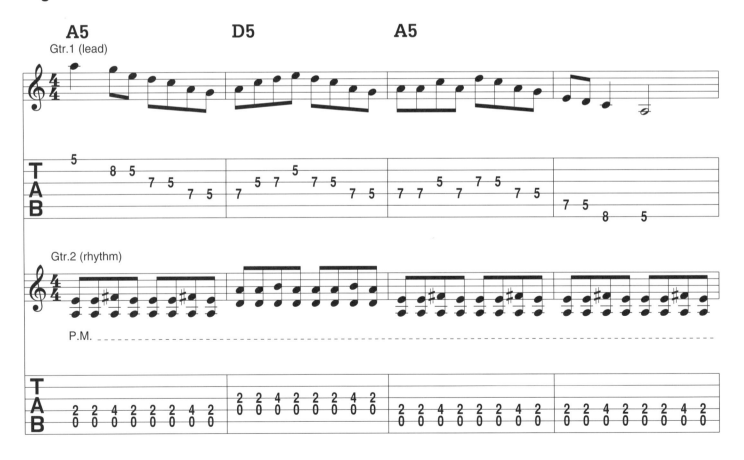

Figure 43 (continued)

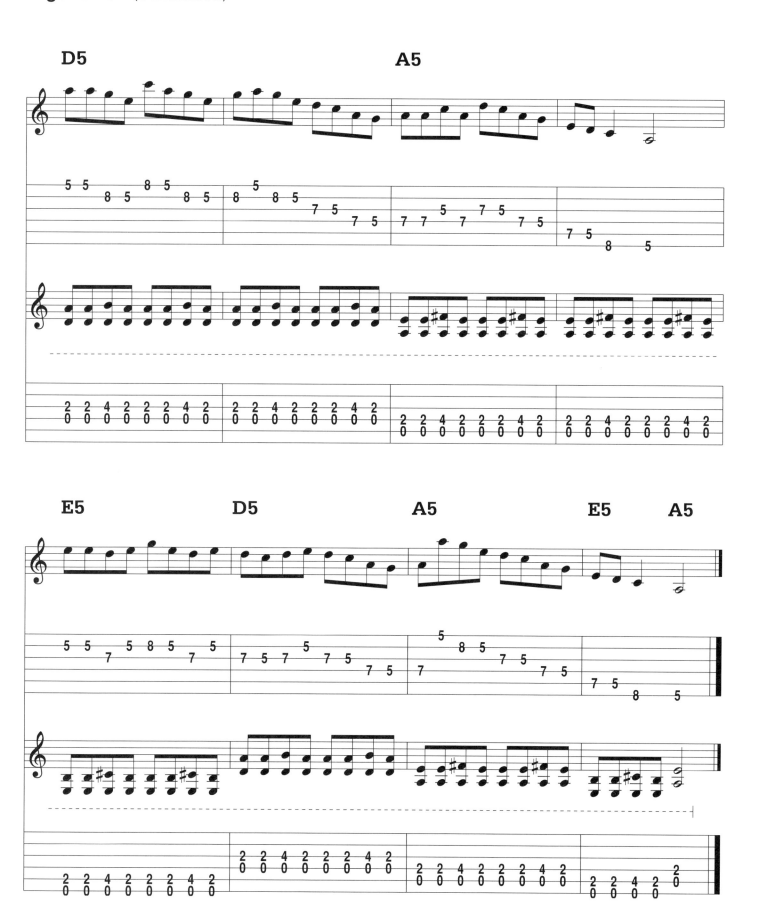

Playing Along With Records

Another great way to learn how to play rhythm and lead is to just play along with your favorite tape or CD. This is one of the fastest ways to train your ears and fingers! Start with a simple song. Try to figure out the main riff or just jam along with it. The more you do this, the better you'll become!

Promotion Certificate

This is to certify that

has successfully completed **Beginning Rock Guitar For Kids** and has

mastered all the techniques and examples presented in the course.

_____
Student Signature

_____
Date

_____
Teacher or Parent Signature

_____
Date

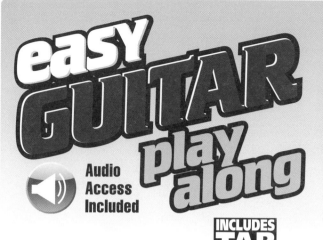

Audio Access Included

INCLUDES TAB

The *Easy Guitar Play Along*® series features streamlined transcriptions of your favorite songs. Just follow the tab, listen to the audio to hear how the guitar should sound, and then play along using the backing tracks. Playback tools are provided for slowing down the tempo without changing pitch and looping challenging parts. The melody and lyrics are included in the book so that you can sing or simply follow along.

1. ROCK CLASSICS
Jailbreak • Living After Midnight • Mississippi Queen • Rocks Off • Runnin' Down a Dream • Smoke on the Water • Strutter • Up Around the Bend.
00702560 Book/CD Pack....... $14.99

2. ACOUSTIC TOP HITS
About a Girl • I'm Yours • The Lazy Song • The Scientist • 21 Guns • Upside Down • What I Got • Wonderwall.
00702569 Book/CD Pack....... $14.99

3. ROCK HITS
All the Small Things • Best of You • Brain Stew (The Godzilla Remix) • Californication • Island in the Sun • Plush • Smells Like Teen Spirit • Use Somebody.
00702570 Book/CD Pack....... $14.99

4. ROCK 'N' ROLL
Blue Suede Shoes • I Get Around • I'm a Believer • Jailhouse Rock • Oh, Pretty Woman • Peggy Sue • Runaway • Wake Up Little Susie.
00702572 Book/CD Pack....... $14.99

6. CHRISTMAS SONGS
Have Yourself a Merry Little Christmas • A Holly Jolly Christmas • The Little Drummer Boy • Run Rudolph Run • Santa Claus Is Comin' to Town • Silver and Gold • Sleigh Ride • Winter Wonderland.
00101879 Book/CD Pack......... $14.99

7. BLUES SONGS FOR BEGINNERS
Come On (Part 1) • Double Trouble • Gangster of Love • I'm Ready • Let Me Love You Baby • Mary Had a Little Lamb • San-Ho-Zay • T-Bone Shuffle.
00103235 Book/
    Online Audio..........$17.99

9. ROCK SONGS FOR BEGINNERS
Are You Gonna Be My Girl • Buddy Holly • Everybody Hurts • In Bloom • Otherside • The Rock Show • Santa Monica • When I Come Around.
00103255 Book/CD Pack.....$14.99

10. GREEN DAY
Basket Case • Boulevard of Broken Dreams • Good Riddance (Time of Your Life) • Holiday • Longview • 21 Guns • Wake Me up When September Ends • When I Come Around.
00122322 Book/
    Online Audio........$16.99

11. NIRVANA
All Apologies • Come As You Are • Heart Shaped Box • Lake of Fire • Lithium • The Man Who Sold the World • Rape Me • Smells Like Teen Spirit.
00122325 Book/
    Online Audio........ $17.99

13. AC/DC
Back in Black • Dirty Deeds Done Dirt Cheap • For Those About to Rock (We Salute You) • Hells Bells • Highway to Hell • Rock and Roll Ain't Noise Pollution • T.N.T. • You Shook Me All Night Long.
14042895 Book/
    Online Audio........ $17.99

14. JIMI HENDRIX – SMASH HITS
All Along the Watchtower • Can You See Me • Crosstown Traffic • Fire • Foxey Lady • Hey Joe • Manic Depression • Purple Haze • Red House • Remember • Stone Free • The Wind Cries Mary.
00130591 Book/
    Online Audio........$24.99

HAL•LEONARD®
www.halleonard.com

Prices, contents, and availability subject to change without notice.